Love Poems
to
No One

Romantic Poetry

by

N.R. Hart

Monday Creek Publishing
Ohio USA

My poetry belongs to the
midnight moon a lover's
chase shattered stars and
lonely hearts. My poetry
belongs to you. - N.R.Hart

A Winter Season

"Everything I never told you
lives inside me."

N.R.Hart

"perhaps you are
a romantic
like me
one who loves
with their soul."

-N.R.Hart

Close your eyes
imagine me
loving you...
the flutter of butterflies
feel my soul...
needing you wanting you
touching you...
pleading in breathless
whispers...
aching for your love.

-N.R.Hart "ache"

And I have stopped
looking for you
because I know you
now live inside me.
You are the warmth
in my veins, you are
every breath I take,
you are the chaos
in my mind.
Now when I look at me,
you are all I see.

-N.R.Hart

"Ancient Ruins"

Somewhere along the way she had forgotten
who she was, she made herself appear duller
afraid to spread her wings so she could
blend in like the rest of them.
Until one day she realized she wasn't like the rest
of them.
She always knew deep down she felt different
from the start after all, her soul was born
from ancient ruins...
She would use this oh so tender heart and sapient
old soul of hers to move the world in tiny
magnificent ways.
Never let others determine your fate, once she
learned how to soar, those that made her feel small
well, she didn't care what they thought at all.

-N.R.Hart

She was not from
here I was sure of
it...
she was ethereal
fiery, romantic...
maybe she was
a star or the moon
or the sea.

-N.R.Hart

HAVE YOU EVER MET
SOMEONE BEFORE AND
SUDDENLY THEY FEEL
STRANGELY FAMILIAR TO
YOU BUT IT IS THE
FIRST TIME YOU HAVE
MET
ONLY...IT IS NOT THE
FIRST TIME YOUR SOULS
HAVE MET BEFORE.

N.R.HART

I know you feel it too.
The sound of our bodies
falling into each other
again and again...
and how we can never stop
that crashing sound.
The problem is darling,
you are gone and
we are still falling.
-N.R.Hart

I went back
to our favorite spot
to find what
I could not see
the hardest goodbye
in your eyes
the last place
you loved me.
-N.R.Hart

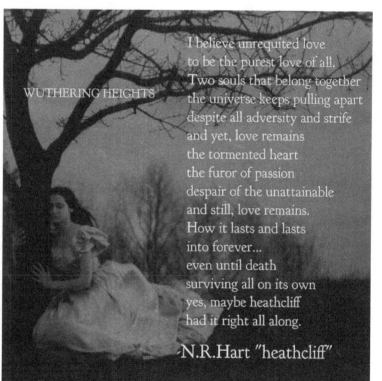

WUTHERING HEIGHTS

I believe unrequited love
to be the purest love of all.
Two souls that belong together
the universe keeps pulling apart
despite all adversity and strife
and yet, love remains
the tormented heart
the furor of passion
despair of the unattainable
and still, love remains.
How it lasts and lasts
into forever...
even until death
surviving all on its own
yes, maybe heathcliff
had it right all along.

N.R.Hart "heathcliff"

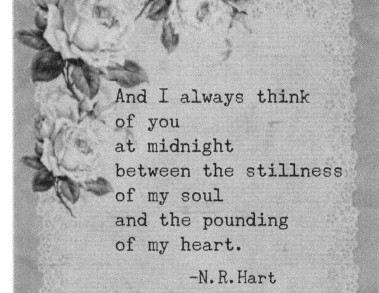

And I always think
of you
at midnight
between the stillness
of my soul
and the pounding
of my heart.

-N.R.Hart

i burn for you
like you are
the sun
and wish for you
like you are
the moon.

-N.R.Hart "sun&moon"

It is very beautiful
isn't it
how much love
we hold onto
even in our darkest hour
when everything else
inside us is dying
we somehow,
keep love alive.
                    -N.R.Hart

I was more myself
with you
than I have ever been
before...
A butterfly freed
from its cocoon
A wildflower dancing
in the wind
A shooting star unfurled
in your arms.

                    -N.R.Hart

We are all or nothing,
the sun and the moon
the beauty and the chaos
the calm before the storm.
We love like there is no tomorrow
and when tomorrow comes
where has the love gone...
it was pure madness...but one we could not
do without
the most we had ever felt.
And, just like a force of nature
the extreme elements are always unpredictable
my darling, just like love...
with love and hate so closely
intertwined, it is either all or nothing
And yet...it is everything. -N.R.Hart *"love and hate"*

Love me hard
break me into
a million pieces
then love me
back together
again.
-N.R.Hart

And, that's the difference
between me and you.
I spend my entire lifetime
loving...
and you, you think you have
an entire lifetime
to love.
You don't. Love now.

-N.R.Hart

Love Story

Sometimes you don't realize
what something truly means
to you until you are ready
to fight for it time and time
again.
Nothing ever came easy for us
but being with you was so damn
easy.
We fought and hung on for dear
life to the story of you and me.
And it's true, our love story
may not have been an easy one
but, all the truly great ones...
They never are.   -N.R.Hart

I feel your absence in my bones
a dull brittle ache lurking...
until it becomes loud at times
like a sharp shooting pain
piercing my heart.
And, what of my melancholy soul?
It is heartbroken...
roaming inside my body
looking for you.

-N.R.Hart "melancholy soul"

Pillow talk - part2

And, midnight can be the
hardest time of day...
a heaviness hangs in the air
and the ghosts of darkness
have come to haunt again
reminding us of all the love
we have lost...
And, if you listen close enough
you can almost hear your heart
speaking, except most nights
mine is weeping. Weeping for
you.   -N.R.Hart

Silence connects soulmates
in a way words never could
because their souls
were speaking for them.

-N.R.Hart "soulmates"

I love our silences together
how we understand
each other
as our hearts speak.
It feels like warmth.
It feels like love.

-N.R.Hart

And, there is a reason why
you can't walk away
there is a reason why you
stay.
It is because we belonged
to each other from the start.
You don't know this but
we secretly rescue each other...
from life, from love, from
everything.
Your soul and my soul are
the same.
We exist in each other.
And, the only thing scarier
than staying is leaving because
our souls already knew we
could never part. -N.R.Hart
"Souls"

His hands were strong
when she wanted
and gentle when she needed
and somehow he knew
the difference.

-N.R.Hart

There is a fear in being
too vulnerable in love
because it will only lead
to heartbreak...
but I would rather feel
everything
than feel nothing
and I would rather stay soft
in this hard world
because my heart is not afraid
because my heart only knows
how to love this way...
And, I would break my own heart
just to love you harder.
And, I would stop time just
to love you longer.

-N.R.Hart

There was just something
dangerous about you
that caused me to breathe
differently
in your presence...
I never knew whether to
hold my breath or lose it
completely.

-N.R.Hart

She wanted to feel it all
everything that was
meant for her...
the passion the pain
the beauty the heartache
the love...
she knew once
she stopped feeling
vulnerable
she would stop feeling
her soul...
And a soul is a beautifully
human thing.   - N.R. Hart

She doesn't want
the prince
on a white horse
from the storybook
she wants a warrior
in armor of black
smelling of war and
moonlight
fighting for love
with a sword of fire
and her...on his back.

-N.R.Hart "sword of fire"

She always wanted it to be him
as she glanced down at her phone
haphazardly wishing that it would
be him this time...
And when it finally was him she could
barely contain her excitement...
she immediately felt flushed, catching
her breath, her heart fluttering and skipping
its beats.
She did not fully understand his effect on her
all she knew was just one word from him and
she was immediately transported back into
their own little world again...
What was this stronghold over her and how she
could not deny him.
Her body betrayed her as she trembled with his
every word sending shockwaves of desire
through her....
she just couldn't help herself...
She had a weakness for him
an ache for his touch a longing
for his kiss.
He was just something she couldn't
resist. -N.R.Hart "irresistible"

I don't want to stop
writing about us
don't you see?
If I stop writing
about us it will mean
the death of you and me.
-N.R.Hart

We sat there in
silence   trying
to tell each other
how we felt
yet your eyes told
me everything...
for I already knew   that
you loved me too.
-N.R.Hart

I won't tell you how love is supposed to be,
because truth is...love is many things,
least of all predictable.
It is feeling things we shouldn't and not feeling
things we should.
It is unexplainable at times, leaving us at a loss
for words...
It involves the heart, a wild creature...and insists
on feeling what it wants when it wants.
As much as we try to control our own hearts,
they will control us instead.
Because, love is many things, it is confusing
and complicated and messy and beautiful...
but mostly, love is breathtaking in all its wildly
undeniable, unshaken glory.

-N.R.Hart "wild creature"

A Spring Season

"My heart still speaks of our fire."

N.R.Hart

Why does love only
come alive
in-between these
lines...
I pause to breathe
you in
write another word
learn another rhyme
compose another stanza
And, love is reborn
again.
        -N.R.Hart

    "a poet and her muse"

His strength is my weakness
his armor my shield
rough around the edges
with a smooth talking tongue
just enough bad to bring
a good girl to her knees.
The power to break me
then love me back together
again.

-N.R.Hart

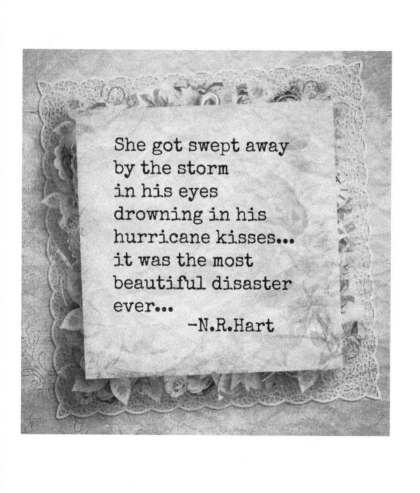

She got swept away
by the storm
in his eyes
drowning in his
hurricane kisses...
it was the most
beautiful disaster
ever...
                    -N.R.Hart

His hands on her
touching her knowing her...
his eyes raking over her
his fingers running through
her soul
she finds it hard to breathe
she felt powerless
within his tight grip
as he stole her every
breath...
and she wonders to herself
with him on this earth...
will she ever breathe normally
again?

-N.R.Hart

Clearly, they were in love
with each other...
he was looking at her and
she was staring back at him
and they were talking and
laughing and blushing...
like the best of friends.
Clearly, they were in love
with each other.
Everyone could see it.
Everyone...but them.

-N.R.Hart

He leaned over and kissed
her...
her mouth crushing against his
she wound her hands
around his neck possessively
her fingers running through
the thickness of his hair
she liked the roughness of him
as if to say...this is mine or I
want this to be mine or this will be
mine.
Then the sweet kiss
the hammering of her heart
the rushing of heat to her ears
making her breathless
her body on fire.
And, she wasn't entirely certain
she would even survive it all.

-N.R.Hart "mine"

But, something was different
that night
as the stars shivered
between us...
your kiss lingered this time
saying goodnight...
How was I to know
it would be goodbye
instead?

(I would have kept kissing you
longer deeper harder always forever)

-N.R.Hart "goodnight"

"hello goodbye"

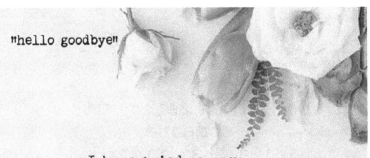

I have tried so many
times to say goodbye
but they always seem
to turn into hello
and I still haven't
figured out how
to let you go.

                    -N.R.Hart

Sometimes being with
someone
feels so right
that your storms fall
silent
and you are at peace
the inner turmoil is just
your soul trying
to find its home.

-N.R.Hart

I just love you. I do.
The way you understand me
when no one else does.
Your smile, how it teases me.
I like the sexy way you look
at me.
And, I like how you feel
when I am touching you.
I like you. And, I just really
love you. I do.

                              -N.R.Hart

She waits for the indigo sky
to appear clearing the afternoon
cool blues and muted violets
she recalls his smile
illuminating the heavens...
she wishes for it now.
And his eyes, she still feels on her
a starry sea washing over her
how many times she has lived
just to drown inside those eyes....
He comes to her in crystal waves
filmy and sublime like a dream
she still believes in...
Maybe she is naive to keep hope
alive...if only she could forget
his smile crashing into her world
and the sweetness of his lips
crushing hers. If only. - N.R. Hart

Let yourself fall
for what you love
allowing fear to stop you
is just a useless emotion
that keeps you from doing
what you feel
just keep falling...
even if you end up
scattered on the ground
you can pick yourself up
knowing you loved
breathtakingly, unregrettably
with every piece of you.

-N.R.Hart

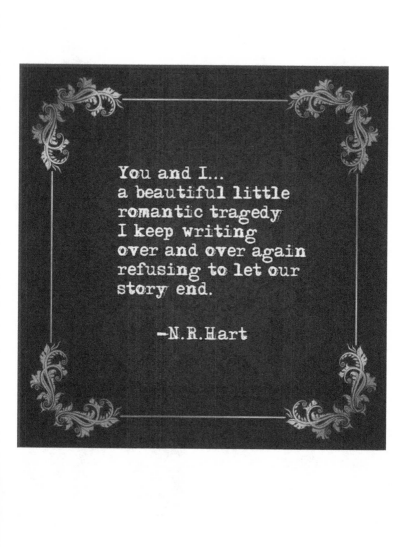

You and I...
a beautiful little
romantic tragedy
I keep writing
over and over again
refusing to let our
story end.

—N.R.Hart

He was my armor
I was his heart.
He was my strength
I was his weakness.
He was my safe
I was his wild.
And, together we were
some sort of strange
beautiful magic.

-N.R.Hart "strange beautiful"

What is this ache inside
that keeps me wanting
more...
And I can't seem to forget
the hunger in your eyes
and the way they devour me
or maybe it's the way
I need my hands on you
and how I can't seem to stop
touching you
because it's you, I want to
keep looking at
and it's you, whose eyes
I want on me.
This love is still burning
somewhere inside me...
You are all I see. -N.R.Hart

and, i don't know what

we talk about really

just being near you

is enough

our hearts smiling

your soul touching mine.

–N.R.Hart

She buried her head
into his shoulder
and stayed there
for the longest time.
She held on tight
hoping he could feel
just how much
she needed him.

-N.R.Hart

And, broken hearts keep
beating just the same
even while breaking
even in pieces...
you can never silence love.
Not ever.

-N.R.Hart

Your words float
inside my head
warming me
like a daydream
I awaken
to my nightmare
you are not here.

And all I want is
to stay
wherever you are.

        - N.R.Hart

She's a romantic
with a pounding heart
she doesn't wait
for tomorrow
it may never come
she lives in the moment
a flurry of butterflies
intoxication
she wants love
and hope
and you and now
and now.   —N. R. Hart

I thought if I kept writing about you that
I would run out of words. Yet, these words
are still breathing, they are living inside me
making a home.
I keep searching hard for the right words.
The words that will mean something to you,
hit you in just the right way. The ones you
won't ever forget. The words you will
always remember.
The ones that make you stay.
To be us again. To love with one
last breath again. Because, you are
still burning somewhere inside me
and my heart...it still speaks of our fire."

-N.R.Hart "fire"

she liked him. she did.
he had wild hair and an
old soul like hers and
somehow she had fallen
tragically
in love
with his sad beautiful
eyes.

-N.R.Hart

"sad.beautiful"

He put his hands on her
pulling her towards him
as he hoarsely whispered
"I am going to make you mine..."
and upon hearing those words
they elicited such a response
in her
so strong and binding
she felt her soul leave her body
as she became his.
A possession so sweet,
so otherworldly...
it overtakes you, it becomes you
And nothing else exists in
this world.
Nothing but this love. This fire.

-N.R.Hart "otherworldly"

The way your eyes
make me shiver
shatter every part
of my soul
how they linger on me
seduce and undress me
make love to me
the way your eyes
hypnotize and control
how they make me come alive
and I have lived and died
inside your eyes.
                    -N.R.Hart

and, you were quite mistaken
thinking you could replace
our passion
with a lukewarm love
so close your eyes
and feel me
covering your body with my lips
on those nights you are left
wanting more
because a fire like ours comes
once in a lifetime
forever burning your soul.

-N.R.Hart

She was a shy girl
a vulnerable girl locked inside
her own little world
she loved deeply though
and if she loved you
you would know...
yes, she didn't show her heart
to many
she never wanted you
to go away
but it was her eyes
always her eyes begging you
to stay...   -N.R.Hart

"stay"

Remember when I was yours
I cannot forget
under this shaded sycamore tree
the quiet wind blows your memory
through my bones
so sweet your honeysuckle taste
your kiss sinking deeper
into my mouth
and how we tasted the same
a warm chill sits on my skin
where your fingers rested once
as my heart hurries towards yours
beneath this tree to remember you
as you forget me.
-N.R.Hart

Call me a romantic
as I throw caution
to the wind...
but I would rather be
running towards something
towards you...
than running away.

-N.R.Hart

It happens once in a lifetime
a divine meeting between souls
fated and predestined
by the universe
an encounter so right it feels like
home.
It's your soul falling in love
with another soul.
Pay attention it happens only once
and never again.

-N.R.Hart "twinflame"

N.R.Hart

"She craves a strong hand
and a tender heart
a warrior lover...
a beast of a man who can
feel her and possess her
in the way she needs
to be loved." -N.R.Hart

But a passionate love
is never a calm love.
It is storms and
chaos
lightning and thunder.
A wildfire burning
out of control.

-N.R.Hart

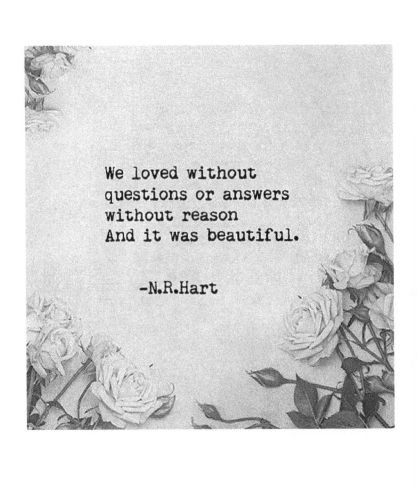

We loved without
questions or answers
without reason
And it was beautiful.

-N.R.Hart

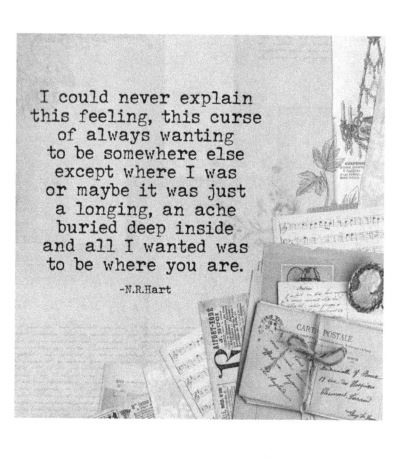

I could never explain
this feeling, this curse
of always wanting
to be somewhere else
except where I was
or maybe it was just
a longing, an ache
buried deep inside
and all I wanted was
to be where you are.

-N.R.Hart

A Summer Season

"Give me that kind of love.
The kind poets write of.."

N.R.Hart

I keep you close
to my heart.
It beats stronger
with you there.

-N.R.Hart

she wanted a man
who would surrender
his soul to her
and at the same time
leave her conquered.

-N.R.Hart "conquered"

CRASH AND BURN

HE WANTED TO KISS HER
AND SHE TOO WANTED TO KISS HIM
BADLY...
EVERY TIME SHE LOOKED INTO
HIS EYES THEY REMINDED HER
OF THE SUN, SOMETHING WAS
BURNING IN THERE...
SHE COULDN'T HELP FLIRTING
WITH DANGER DARING LOVE
TO SMOULDER AGAINST HER LIPS
CRASH AND BURN
INSIDE HIS KISS.   - N.R. HART

I crave a beautiful tragedy
a love story to remember
trembling hearts
soul on soul love
make love to my mind
manhandle my body
move me consume me
love me break me
love me again...
Intoxicate me with your mouth.
I want to get drunk on you.
Drunk on love.

N.R.Hart / "drunk'

i don't fall often
but when i do
it's fast and hard
it's breathtaking
and forever.

-N.R.Hart "fall"

your skin was touching mine
and it felt like fire
against me
we were melting into
one another
so close until we absorbed
into each other
I was you and you were me
and we were together
finally.

-N.R.Hart "finally"

she couldn't help but inch
a little closer to him
he was fire...
and oh how she longed
to stay warm.

-N.R.Hart

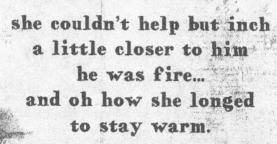

And, this love
is ours
and, this love
belongs only
to us
oh, how this love
has a heartbeat
all its own.

-N.R.Hart

My heart was
hungry
for him
hungry for his
kind of love.

-N.R.Hart

I like the way
you look at me
like you are
about to talk
to me
or devour me
and I am fine
with either.

-N.R.Hart

Longing

Her lips brushed softly
against his
he caressed her cheek
held her hair in his hands
sending shivers down
her spine
how they trembled
for each other...
maybe this wasn't forever
but this was a longing
neither of them could deny
and both of them knew
they weren't leaving each
other tonight. —N.R.Hart

She was in love
with his mind
his words were
all she could hear
Taking her to the
edge of madness...
always touching her
even when he was not
near.

-N.R.Hart / "madness"

I knew the moment
you kissed hot poems
into my ravenous mouth
and wrote lyrical sonnets
onto my bare skin
my heart would be forever
ravaged by you
shattered and rewritten
into fresh new verses
for I could not turn from
your scintillating fragments
forever piercing my soul.

- N.R. Hart

"poems & sonnets"

Do you remember
that night
we loved like
burning stars
we loved without words
we loved in the dark
we loved violently
in pure moonlight.
-N.R.Hart

she is an exquisite
girl
who loves with reckless
abandon
and she kisses like
there is no tomorrow
she will love you until
the bittersweet end
and smile at
love's
beautiful wreckage.

-N.R.Hart

Darkness falls and I become
something else
my heart aches for love...
and I become like the night
blood thirsty and howling
underneath the moon
for my lover.

-N.R.Hart

Something about that night
still burns in my memory...
maybe it was the way
I tasted your soul
in my mouth on that warm
summer night
or how you placed moonlight
in my hair setting me on fire
or even the way I carved
my body into yours
kissing you long and deep
like you were my salvation
and I was starving
I cannot forget...
and I can still
taste you there. N.R.Hart

There are some days
I am surviving without you
and on other days
the waves of you
come crashing down
hard upon me and I am
drenched
in the sea of your memory.

-N.R.Hart

She was waiting
for she didn't
know what
exactly... maybe
a fairytale ending
a storybook love
a wicked romance
novel or all
of the above.

N.R.HART

"Soulmates"

Soulmates aren't just anyone you meet.
They are souls you instantly have a
connection with.
They are souls who know you better than
you sometimes know yourself.
They are the ones who can almost hear your
thoughts without you uttering a word.
You find comfort in their presence and you
are understood in their silence.
They represent love and danger and you
come alive with them near.
You ache to know everything about them.
You have a longing to know them.

-N.R.Hart

"Starving hearts"

He had that wild look
in his eyes again
one she recognized all too well
and said "we are the same,
you know.."
part human part animal
starving hearts hungry mouths
he said "show me" so she gathered
him up kissed him tenderly then
devoured him.   -N.R.Hart

Meeting your twin flame will not
be a chance encounter but rather
your souls will recognize one another.
You will know it by how you feel
because you won't feel that way
with anyone but them.
Everything feels different, looks
different, is different.
The connection is so strong
and intense it may even scare
you....but you will not be able to
ignore it. You come alive around them
and the passion you experience
is out of control almost to the brink
of madness. And it is the most you
have ever felt.
You breathe differently now and every cell
inside you is on fire, and yet
they bring you a kind of peace you have
never known.
Your entire world is shaken..and yet
you are home. -N.R.Hart "twin flame"

I am not waiting
for an ordinary love.
I am waiting for our kind of love.
The kind that makes you feel
like you are dying and fully alive
at the same time.
The ache of never getting enough...
hands and mouths everywhere.
The one that makes you feel insane
with wanting and needing...
for you to touch me again.
Take me again. Love me again.
I live for that kind of love.
-N.R.Hart

We were all of it
best friends, lovers
soul mates...
it was never just
about the sex
we made love
every time
our eyes met.

N.R.Hart "Twin Flame"

Girls like her
were made for love
she kept it tightly wound
like a strung wire
about to snap
she was waiting for
the right touch
unbridling her passion
unleashing her love.
-N.R.Hart

You were different
somehow,
I found you
in poems
pieces of my soul
scattered
a word here a verse there
as you held the power
to destroy me
in tiny beautiful ways...
poetic tragic little
vignettes.

                    -N.R.Hart

she has that lost look
in her eyes again
how she tries desperately
to hold onto what
she loves
always staying and
staying...
while their eyes keep
reminding her of
leaving.

—N.R.Hart "lost"

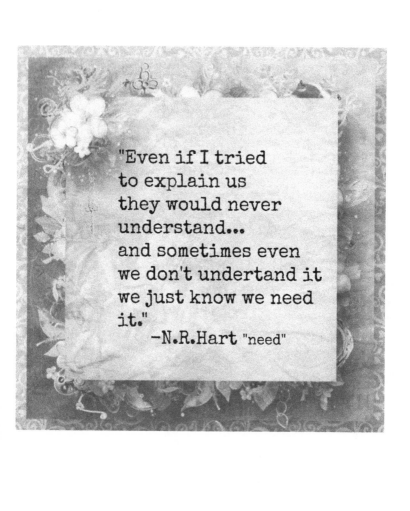

"Even if I tried
to explain us
they would never
understand...
and sometimes even
we don't undertand it
we just know we need
it."
      -N.R.Hart "need"

He is terrifying
and wild.
A wild love.
Something she should
run from.
But...he was beautiful
and made her heart
beat faster
so she stayed instead.
-N.R.Hart

Her body language
was sexy around him
her consuming awareness
of his maleness
the musk and moss of him
a heady fragrance delicately
sinking into her skin
she was fascinated
by his effect on her
she could not will herself
to look away
craving his kiss...
wildly wanting him to stay.

-N.R.Hart, musk and moss

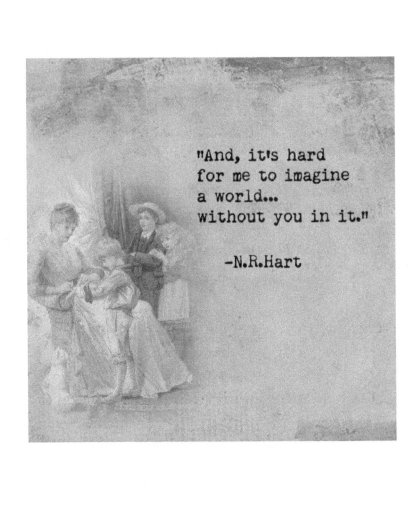

"And, it's hard
for me to imagine
a world...
without you in it."

-N.R.Hart

An Autumn Season

"Love me back to life."

N.R.Hart

"coffee shop" poetry

You see, there's this girl
sitting in a corner
of this coffee shop...
and she hasn't moved
she hasn't breathed
just sipping her coffee
barely holding on
waiting for you...
to come back to her
again.
                    -N.R.Hart

She was a divine
contradiction
oh, how she craved
a savage love
the crush of a hard body
with a firm hand
tugging her hair
and clothes
followed by soft
whispers
making love to her soul.

-N.R.Hart

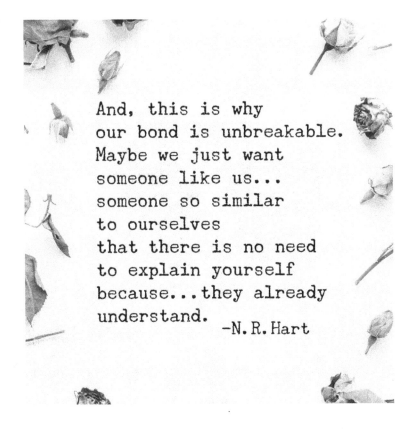

And, this is why
our bond is unbreakable.
Maybe we just want
someone like us...
someone so similar
to ourselves
that there is no need
to explain yourself
because...they already
understand. —N.R.Hart

I sat at my typewriter
with all these thoughts
of you
running through my mind
and the paper stayed
blank...
you are still a language
I have some trouble
learning.

-N.R.Hart "language"

Maybe I am just a
paragraph
in your book separated
by commas in-between
your silences...
and semi-colons during
your distance...
but I will love you until
the very last page.

-N.R.Hart "last page"

She is his dark fairytale
he is her wicked romance
novel
and their love story is what
legends are made of.

-N.R.Hart

And what scares me
the most
what if I never love
like that again...
-N.R.Hart

I wrote these
love letters
with hushed tones
moonlight wishes in pink
prose wondering if you
read them hoping you
might see the words this
poet penned in secret
never the courage
to send.

-N. R. Hart

"Love Poems to No One"

Love's greatest tragedy...
it holds the power to
destroy you and save you...
all at once.

-N.R.Hart "love's greatest tragedy"

All i know is that
i love you
and i don't know how
or when this ensuing
madness that followed
but there is just something
about you
so deeply engrained
underneath my skin
the very thought of you
I come completely
undone.
And, i love you.
                    -N.R.Hart

And, that was her
magic
finding the words
for you...
the ones you never
knew how to speak

-N.R.Hart

It had everything
to do with how
you made me feel.
I was different
with you
and you felt it too.
I was more me and you
were more you.

-N.R.Hart "more"

It is a rare thing when
something moves you,
so when it does
you must move with it.
Cross the oceans the stars
cross the lines...
anything to follow
the heat of passion
Love fiercely love passionately
we are only here
for a short while...
love boldly love breathlessly.
Love...while you still can.
-N.R.Hart

Mulberry Love

I believed you when you said
you felt our souls touching
as our breaths became one
and how your roots knotted
themselves inside my hair
as you twisted your body
in-between my limbs
chasing shadows from my heart
all I see is your face
and scream your name
as you kiss sweet poems
down my throat
mulberry lust burning love
till we both taste the same.

  – N. R. Hart

This heart of mine has
been through too much...
too much love
too much sadness
too much hope
too much breaking
so if you are in my life
and i love you
then i need for you to stay.
My heart...
needs you to stay.
                    -N.R.Hart

he took her
immediately
his hands warm upon her skin
his fingers buried deep
inside her
she whimpered with every
stroke
he knew just how to touch her
he knew just how to kiss her
he knew just how to
love her
back to life.

-N.R.Hart

Always the poet
never a poem
always the romantic
never a romance
always the lover
never a love.
Maybe it is time for her
to be alive again.
-N.R.Hart

The wind nearly swept
up my poetry today
as I clutched it
ever so dearly
to my heart
you see, if the wind
had carried it away...
you would be gone too.
Since poetry is all
I have left of you.

-N.R.Hart "october winds"

Of all the love poems
I have written
you are my favorite one.
They are all about you
for you, to you
with you...
There is only one you
and only one love story.

— n.r. hart

One day, I will find
the right words
to describe these
feelings...
and I will no longer
be grasping for things
I have no name for.

-N.R.Hart

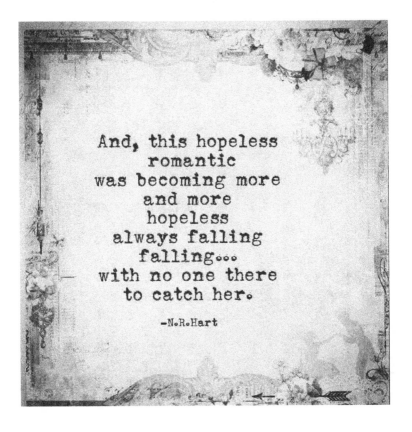

And, this hopeless
romantic
was becoming more
and more
hopeless
always falling
falling...
with no one there
to catch her.

-N.R.Hart

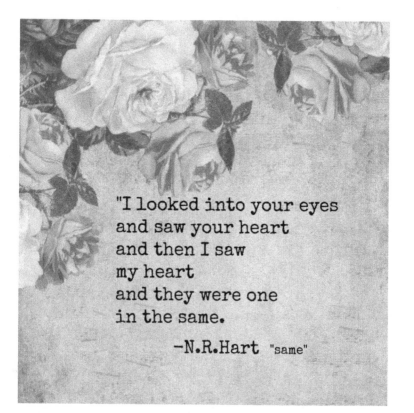

"I looked into your eyes
and saw your heart
and then I saw
my heart
and they were one
in the same.

—N.R.Hart "same"

i only know that when you
kissed me
my entire world changed.
i now lived in this secret
world somewhere between
heaven and hell
where
i was burning alive.

-N.R.Hart "world"

She wonders if he lies awake
thinking of her like she is
thinking of him.
She wonders about kissing him
and other wild things in the dead
of night.
And how can two people think
this much about each other
she can't help but wonder
and why are they still apart?

-N.R.Hart

stay with me

let us be

whatever we are

supposed

to be.

-N.R.Hart "stay"

I am in love with the innocent ones
the ones who fall in love
with love simply because
they cannot help themselves.
They are the unafraid ones
the ones who love against
all reason
they hold it sacred like
a religion.
These are the ones no matter
how many times their hearts
have shattered and still,
they love more.
This is their charm, a pure heart.
These are the ones I understand.
These are the ones I love.
                              -N.R.Hart

Things I will miss. You.
The way your eyes light up
gives me butterflies every single time.
That smile of yours...
Our last minute road trips hopping in your
car telling you to take me anywhere...
Time never mattered to us
the world disappears when we're together. You.
Midnight texts. Midnight lover
kissing under our midnight moon.
Your charming, disarming smile
that gets you whatever you want. Your hands,
the way they know just how to touch me.
You make me come undone.
Did I mention your smile? I swear it takes
my breath away.
Your hugs, your neck, your body.
The way you felt...
Your touch, your touch, your touch. You.
Our passion, our laughing, our love,
the way you tease me, our friendship.
You, you, you, you. You... N.R. Hart

it will take awhile
this undoing
of you...
from my bones
my blood my soul.

-N.R.Hart

She's the girl who caught you off guard,
isn't she?
She was unexpected and yet she
changed everything.
The kind of girl you fall in love with
and never knew it until it was much
too late.
There is something about her
something different
that makes her completely unexplainable
and yet, it doesn't even matter because
you are going to love her anyway.
And, she is the one who loved you
in such a way that you have never
been loved before, so unapologetically
so shamelessly, herself.
And, now you will see just how
unforgettable this girl can be.   -N.R.Hart

Do not be gentle with me
I need to feel your heart
pumping just for me
the desperation
in your hands
aching to touch me
the hunger in your kiss
dying to taste me
your body penetrating mine
the yearning of two souls
finally united as one.
        -N.R.Hart

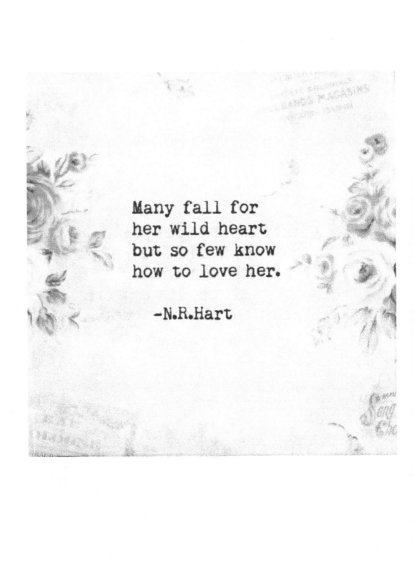

Many fall for
her wild heart
but so few know
how to love her.

-N.R.Hart

Different people
bring out different
worlds in us...
but I fell in love with
all the worlds in you.

-N.R.Hart "worlds"

ABOUT THE AUTHOR

N.R.Hart started writing poetry at a young age and used her poetry as a way to express her innermost thoughts and emotions. A true romantic at heart, she expresses feelings of love, hope, passion, despair, vulnerability and romance in her poetry. Trapping time forever and a keeper of memories is what she loves most about the enduring power of poetry. Her poetry has been so eloquently described as "words delicately placed inside a storm." Poetry is here to make us feel instead of think; as thinking is for the mind and poetry is for the heart and soul. N.R.Hart hopes to open up your heart and touch your soul with her poetry.

"Poetry is not dead, it is alive
in the minds of those
who feel...instead of think."

N.R.Hart

Connect with N.R. Hart:
Facebook@N.R. Hart, Author
Facebook@PearlsSlippingOffAString
Instagram@nrhartpoetry
Tumblr@nrhartpoetry

Printed in the USA
CPSIA information can be obtained
at www.ICGtesting.com
LVHW051250061123
762867LV00003B/7

9 780578 451169